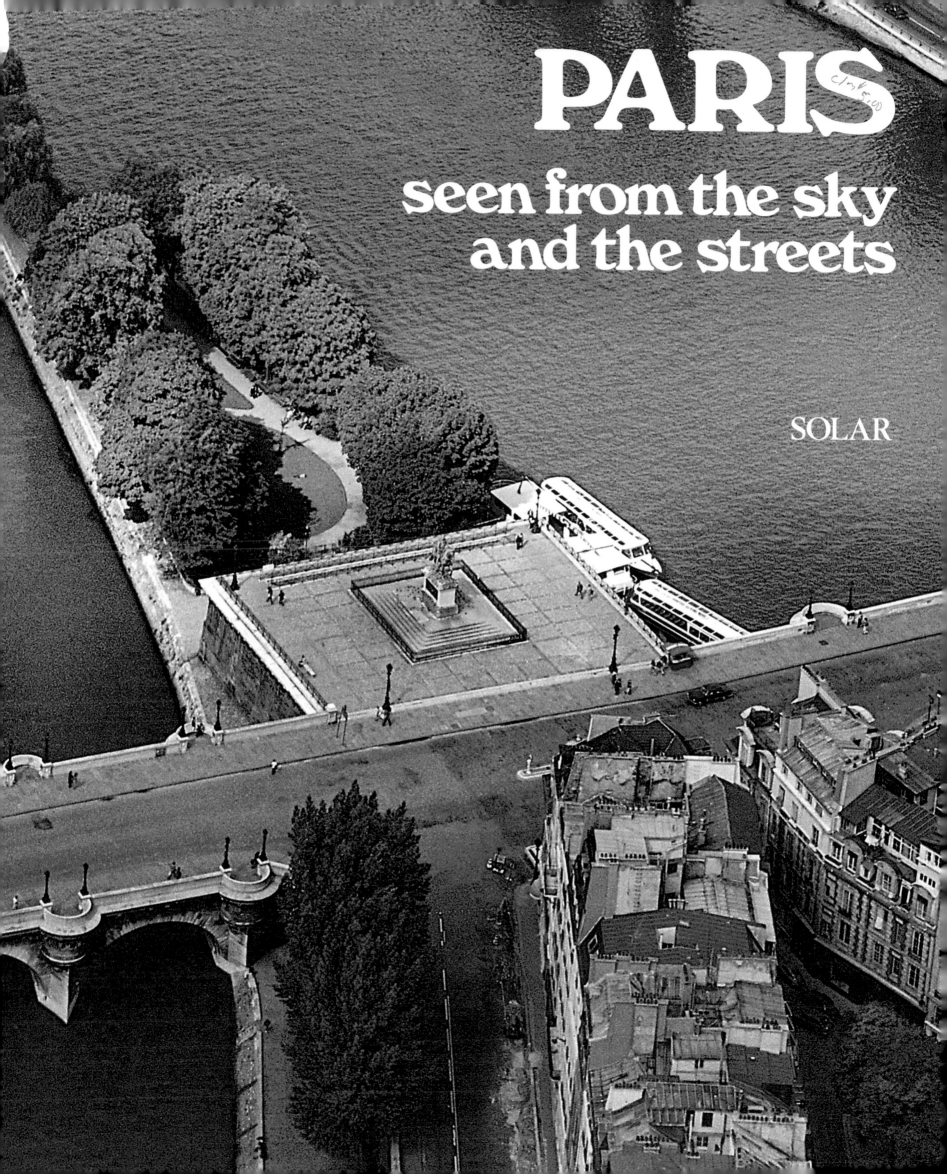

PARIS
seen from the sky and the streets

SOLAR

Designed and produced by
ÉDITIONS MINERVA S.A.

© Éditions Minerva, S.A. Genève, 1986

TEXTS BY ANDRE BOURGUIGNON

Cover : 1. The Trocadéro Palace, the Eiffel Tower and the Military Academy. 2. The Place de la Concorde.
Title-page : the point of the Island of the City, seen from the Pont-Neuf.
End-papers : the Louvre and the Tuileries.

Printed by
Printer Industria Gráfica S.A.
Barcelona - España
D.L.B. 7864-1986
N.° d'éditeur : 1374
ISBN : 2-263-01075-0
Printed in Spain

Let's dream a little . . . It is 21st November 1783 at exactly ten to two in the afternoon, and here in the gardens of the Muette, a huge blue and gold soap-bubble rises slowly into the air. Its bulging form glows resplendently with painted suns and the signs of the zodiac, intertwined with the monogram of Louis XVI. Two men are busily occupied in a light basket hanging beneath the balloon around a gaping mouth, into which flows the blast of hot air rising from a fire of straw kept alive by one of the men, the Marquis d'Arlande. The other man is Pilâtre de Rozier, a young man of twenty seven, fascinated by the glimpse of the future revealed to him through the successful experiments carried out a few months before by some paper-makers of Annonay, the Montgolfier brothers, and promising to deliver man from the weight

of his own body.

They're up! The two companions dazzled and bewildered glide on their way towards the hill of Chaillot, along past the Island of Swans, slowly cross the river Seine, squeezing their way between the Military Academy and the Invalides. The sparks from the burning straw make tiny holes in the paper enfolding the balloon.

"We must land", cries the Marquis, who can see the danger ahead.

"But we can't," replies Pilâtre. "It's impossible. We are over Paris . . ."

And so the flight continues over the town, in an atmosphere of wild enthusiasm and excitement. The two pioneers are to touch down a few moments later amongst

Left, the Seine in the heart of Paris. Above, a view of the Tuileries Gardens.

the windmills on the Butte-aux-Cailles. The first aerial flight has lasted exactly twenty-six minutes. And what is more, over Paris, if you please! A fabulous dream, which only the Turgot plan had until then made possible, by entrusting the town to the pencil of an artist transported through the air by nothing but the mere force of his imagination.

At that time it was not Cyrano, carried towards the Moon by a whole series of ruses and contraptions that came to mind but rather Lesage's famous "Limping Devil", making use of his magic powers to take one of his students high up above the houses, whose roofs he lifted off, disclosing all the hidden mysteries, both great and small, of his protégé's home town.

Photography has done even better since then, by revealing to us a plan which goes far beyond the mere lay-out of the streets:

the plan of a living city. Of a city whose historical monuments, those vast milestones measuring out the distance through the legends of centuries, are no longer the only way of measuring: with 7,500,000 visitors annually, modern art and the Georges Pompidou Centre can boast well over double the figure for the Eiffel Tower (3,500,000) and the Louvre (3,000,000), leaving far behind the Musée Grévin (600,000), the Arc de Triomphe (500,000) and the Notre-Dame (460,000).

Certainly, Love does not calculate in this way. And Lutetia will always be Lutetia. Even if the television aerials sticking up like hat-pins from the top of the Eiffel Tower, might make us take Belphegor for the ghost of Philip Augustus hovering in the basements of the Louvre . . .

But let us follow the guide. It is still Asmodeus who leads the way.

The Island of the City is shaped like a cradle. In the 3rd century BC, the tribe of the Pariisiis settled here and gave birth to Lutetia. Today 2,800,000 inhabitants live in its 105 square kilometers. Its 4,082 streets cover a distance of 1,354 kilometers and a million and a half cars weave their way in and out of them each morning.

Above : a view from Notre-Dame, looking towards the Gare de Lyon and Bercy. Below : Saint-Louis Island.

Built on the site of a first-century pagan temple, Notre-Dame has dominated the history of France for a thousand years. 130 metres long and 60 metres high, the cathedral can hold 9,000 people. A bronze star set into the parvis marks the starting-point of the main routes out of the capital.

Notre-Dame. Details. The Esplanade.

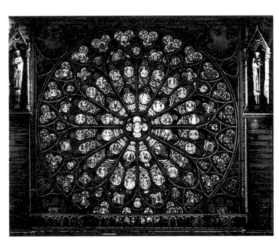

The Palais de Justice, the Conciergerie . . . The Roman governors had already settled here. Saint Louis had the Sainte-Chapelle erected to house the Crown of Thorns worn by Christ. Under the Revolution, these vaults were the antichamber to the guillo-tine for those condemned by the revolutionary courts.

The flower market; the interior of the Ste-Chapelle; the large low hall of the Conciergerie. Right : a view looking down on the Ste-Chapelle; the neo-Gothic façade of the Conciergerie.

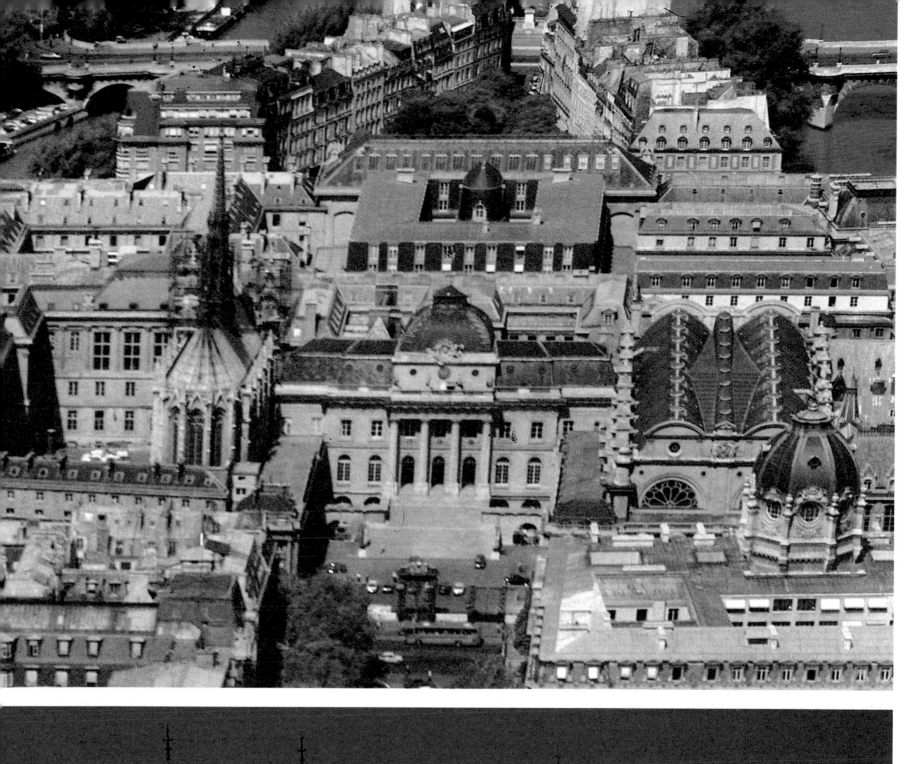

Notre-Dame for the soul, the Hôtel Dieu for the body, the Police Headquarters to discover criminals and the Palais de Justice to mete out the punishment. With Henry IV on horseback, promising a chicken in the pot for everyone, from the top of the Pont-Neuf

Vert-Galant Square; the quayside near the Tuileries; the Pont-Neuf. Right : a general view of the Island of the City; the Vert-Galant seen from different angles; the Pont-Neuf at night.

The Place Dauphine was laid out in 1607 in honour of the Dauphin, the future Louis XIII. It is a delightful little provincial enclave at the end of the Island of the City, a gastronomic haven for the magistrates from the nearby Palais de Justice, extending, beyond the Pont-Neuf, into the Vert-Galant Point, which goes to make up one of the most charming areas of the capital.

The Place Dauphine.

The first castle of the Louvre, built in the year 1200 by Philip Augustus, only occupied a quarter of the present Cour Carrée. The development of the palace closely followed that of France itself right up to the fire at the Tuileries, during the reign of the Commune. The gallery itself was the work of the Convention.

The Louvre and some of its rooms.

The Great Gallery on the banks of the river, 500 metres long, dates from the time of Catherine de Medici. The Arc de Triomphe of the Carrousel was put up in

1805 to celebrate the victories won by Napoleon. Flower-beds with statues by Maillol dotted about amongst them have replaced the Tuileries. The construction of the arcades in the Rue de Rivoli was begun in 1811, and they now line one of the most beautiful thoroughfares in Paris.

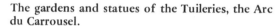

The gardens and statues of the Tuileries, the Arc du Carrousel.

The Tuileries gardens, the Place de la Concorde with the Obelisk, and the Champs-Elysées as far as the Arc de Triomphe at the Etoile, offer over a distance of three kilometers a vista that is unique in the world. This is the route followed by all the great military processions. Children prefer the little boats of the Tuileries.

In series : the Tuileries Gardens, the Obelisk, the Champs-Elysées, the Arc de Triomphe and the towers of the Défense; a hirer of boats and the pool in the Tuileries. Right : the Rue de Rivoli.

The former Place Louis XV only changed its name to "Concorde", as a sign of national reconciliation, after having seen the death of 1,343 victims (including Louis XVI and Marie-Antoinette), who fell beneath the blade of the guillotine. The Louqsor Obelisk was offered to Charles X by the Viceroy of Egypt in the year 1829.

The beauties of the Place de la Concorde.

From Marly's horses right up to the round-about of the Champs-Elysées, the "Champs" shelter under their cool shade a series of embassies, palaces, elegant private residences, theatres and restaurants, all contributing to the atmosphere of discreet distinction suitable to the setting, well protected from the surrounding bustle by solid high-class iron railings.

One end of the Champs-Elysées; the Grand-Palais and the Petit-Palais.

Beneath the extraordinary glass dome which tops its 240 metres of façade, the Grand Palais houses some outstanding exhibitions, while Science has taken over the Palais de la Découverte behind. The Petit Palais belongs to the city of Paris, which has converted it into its Fine Arts Museum. These two buildings have been standing facing each other since the exhibition of 1900, for which they were built, at the same time as the Alexander III bridge.

The Grand- and the Petit-Palais.

The Elysée gardens open out on to the circus through the Cock Gate. The Elysée Palace, the public residence of the Presidents of the Republic since 1873, used to be the home of the Pompadour, the Duchess of Bourbon, serving as the setting for a public ball under the Revolution, before being handed over to Caroline Murat, and later to the Empress Josephine.

The Elysée Palace and an elegant private residence (opposite).

The great fashion-houses are concentrated around the circus. Most notable of the buildings, standing behind a magnificent iron gate, is the building which houses a famous weekly magazine, built originally for a well-known courtesan of the Belle Epoque: la Païva.

The Champs-Elysées Circus, its ornamental lakes and its famous railings; a famous fashion-house in the Avenue Montaigne.

It was Le Nôtre who laid out the Champs-Elysées, between fields and marshes, as a triumphal way for the nation. In spite of its fine fountains and its impressive lighting, the spot remained of rather doubtful reputation until the time when the high society of the Second Empire took to riding there in their elegant coaches and showing themselves off in the fashionable cafés. One of these was the famous Bal Mabille. Nowadays one meets one's friends rather in the luxurious cinemas in the area.

The Champs-Elysées and the Arc de Triomphe. The famous Café "Fouquet's".

The building of the Arc de Triomphe, decided on in 1806 to honour the armies of Napoleon, was only completed in 1836. The famous "Marseillaise" by Rude, decorates one of its sides. The Place de l'Etoile now bears the name of Charles de Gaulle.

Twelve avenues lead off in different directions in a star shape, justifying the earlier name.

The Arc de Triomphe and the Place de l'Etoile or the Place De Gaulle.

Already fashionable at the time when coaches drove through the streets, the Avenue Foch (the broadest in Paris), which leads to the Bois de Boulogne and the Longchamp race-track, remains the most residential in the capital. Other streets lead down towards the Seine or to link up with the areas restored by Haussmann.

Panoramas of the 16th arrondissement; the Longchamp Mill; la Muette and the beginning of the Bois de Boulogne. Right : the Avenue Foch.

"Every man creates without knowing it, as he breathes. But the artist feels himself create, his act involves his whole being. His well-loved pain strengthens him" . . . This quotation from Paul Valéry adorns the Palais de Chaillot, built for the exhibition of 1937 and now housing several museums.

The Palais de Chaillot; the Eiffel Tower, seen from the Palais de Chaillot; the entrance to the Musée de l'Homme; the Trocadéro Gardens.

A controversial subject from its very beginning ("a huge black factory chimney"), fulsomely praised by others (the "sheep-fold of the clouds", according to Apolinaire), this young lady is still very much sought-after, even if she is steadily moving towards her centenary, in 1989.

Different views of the Eiffel Tower.

7,000 tons of steel and 2,500,000 rivets were used in the construction of the Tower which was to take two years, without even the slightest change being made in the plans, perfect as they were from the outset. When the Tower was finished, Gustave Eiffel had an apartment made for him on the third floor, with a breathtaking panoramic view over all the city lying below.

The heart of the Tower. The right bank seen from the Tower.

The Champ-de-Mars stretches from the Tower to the Military Academy. The Revolution held its great Masses to the Goddess Reason there. In later days, the Universal Exhibitions made it the show-case of the nation. The apartments which line it are considered to be amongst the most luxurious in the whole of Paris.

The Military Academy and the Champ-de-Mars.

The Invalides was built to welcome the wounded of the wars of Louis XIV. Napoleon's tomb also receives a considerable number of visitors under Mansart's dome, which stands out as a landmark beyond the Alexander III bridge, as far as the Champs-Elysées.

The Invalides. Above : one of the statues on the roof of the Invalides; below, the Alexander III bridge.

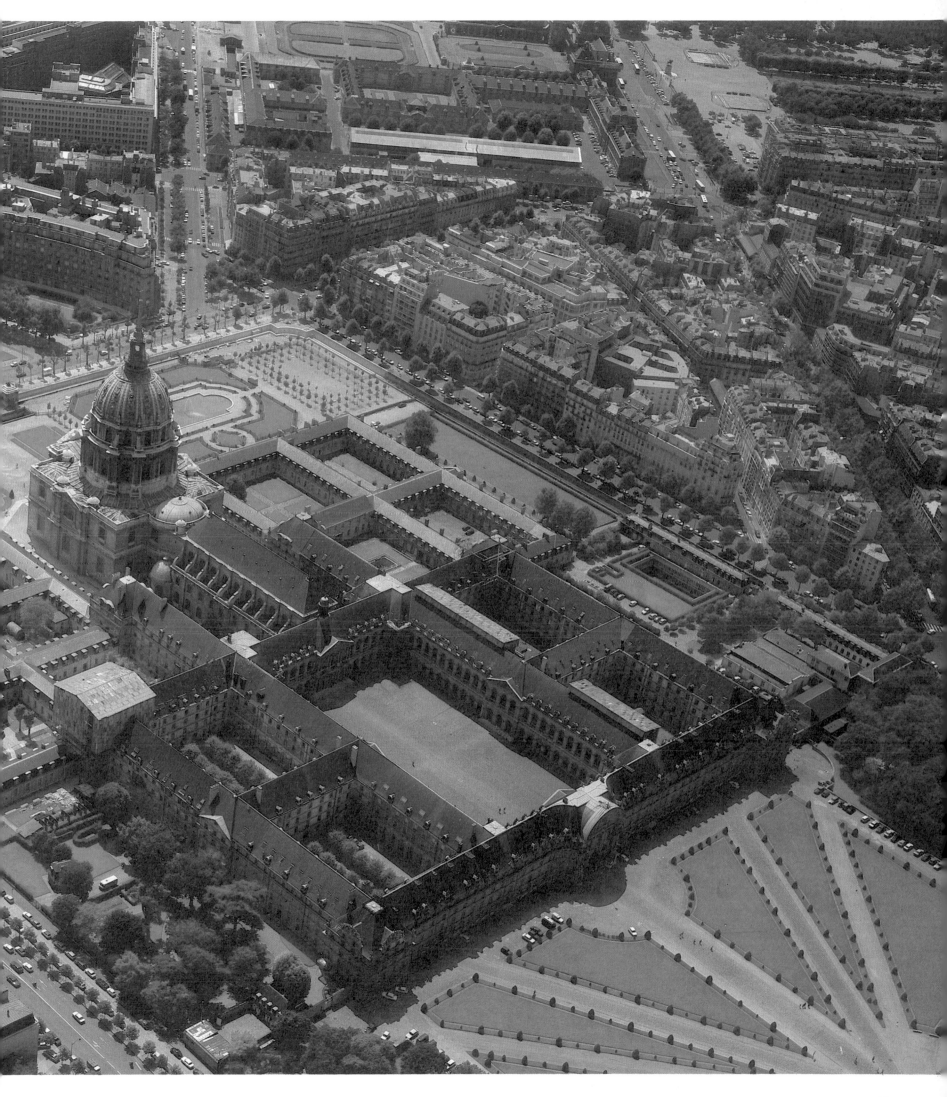

The vista seen from the Concorde is limited on the left bank by the Palais Bourbon, the seat of the National Assembly, whose president lives in the Hôtel de Lassay nearby, next to the imposing Ministry of Foreign Affairs. This is where matters of state are dealt with and French policy decided.

The Palais Bourbon, the Hôtel de Lassay, the Ministry of Foreign Affairs and the Quai d'Orsay.

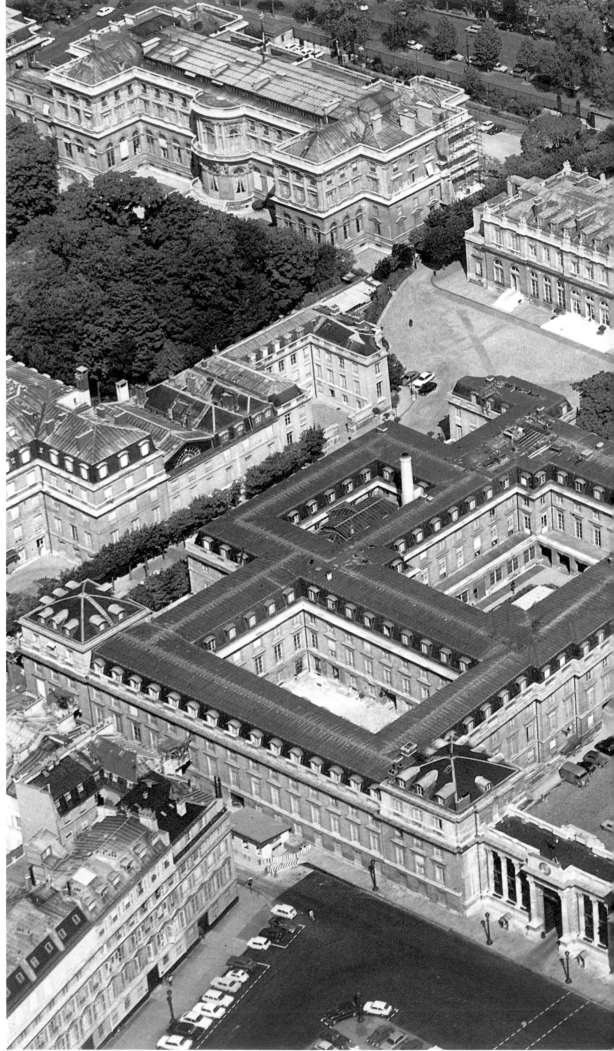

With its rustic church, its square, its "literary" cafés, the market of Buci, the delightful Place Fürstemberg, the towers of St. Sulpice's, its art galleries and its publishers, Saint-Germain-des-Prés is still, as it has always been, the meeting-place for the Parisian intelligentsia, which allows the curious visitor a glimpse of its riches in the fashion shops and restaurants of all kinds.

St-Germain-des-Prés, one of the famous cafés in the square; the Buci market, the Place Fürstemberg; the church of St. Sulpice and its square nearby.

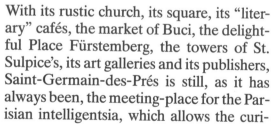

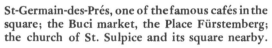

The elegance of the Institute, on the left bank, sets off to perfection the Louvre, which stands facing it, while the Hôtel de la Monnaie, where they no longer strike anything but medals, stretches out at length before the quayside bouquinists.

The footbridge of the Arts and the Institut; the bouquinists along the quays beside the Seine; a view of the Institut from above.

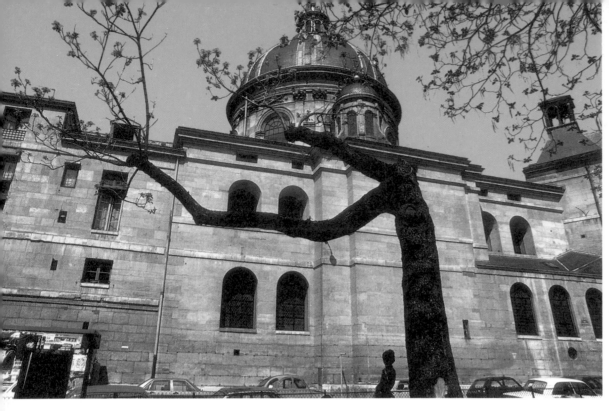

The Académie Française was founded by Richelieu in 1635. The celebrity of its forty members tends to make one forget a little that the famous dome also shelters four other academies: Inscriptions et Belles Lettres, Sciences, Beaux-Arts, Sciences Morales et Politiques.

The Mazarine Library, the dome of the Institut; Conti Quay.

The majestic façade of the Palais du Luxembourg harmonizes completely with the idea of the dignity associated with the senators and their work. The theatre of the Odéon, in the background, is devoted to a different kind of comedy, while, in the most beautiful gardens in Paris, children give themselves up to the pleasures of the puppet-show and the little donkeys.

The Palais du Luxembourg and its gardens. On the right-hand picture, in the background, the Théâtre de l'Odéon.

a paradox! — to emerge from the shade cast upon them by the Tower, 200 metres high, the highest, in fact, in the whole of Europe.

The Maine-Montparnasse Tower and the area around Montparnasse Station.

Town planning has considerably modified the look of the legendary Montparnasse. At the height of their renown in the twen-ties, the great cafés of the Raspail square (the Coupole, the Dôme, the Select) seem to have to wait for the night to dare — what

From the church of St. Peter of Montrouge to the Val-de-Grâce, a whole district spanning the 14th, 6th and 5th arrondissements stands on the Catacombs, in which are piled the bones from the cemetery of the Innocents, closed in 1787.

The Place Maubert; the Val-de-Grâce; the Catacombs; the Avenue du Général Leclerc.

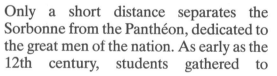

Only a short distance separates the Sorbonne from the Panthéon, dedicated to the great men of the nation. As early as the 12th century, students gathered to exchange their views around the tiny little church of St. Julien-le-Pauvre. The cafés in the Latin Quarter have always had their part to play in the life of the university.

The Panthéon; the rood-screen of the church of St-Etienne-du-Mont; the façade of the Sorbonne and its interior courtyard; the church of St-Julien-le-Pauvre. Right : the Panthéon, the entry to the Musée de Cluny and the Place St-André-des-Arts.

There are in fact two Latin Quarters — that of the educational institutions and the other, very old, taken up by restaurants, cinemas and attractions of all kinds, set around the church of St. Séverin tucked in along the Rue St. Jacques.

The area around the Place St. Michel and the bouquinists along the quays beside the Seine.

Right in the heart of the Châtelet area, the church of St. Jacques-de-la-Boucherie, of which only the tower is still standing, used to be the starting-point for the pilgrimages to Santiago de Compostela. The present Town Hall was entirely rebuilt after the destruction of the former building during the insurrection of the Commune. Under the Ancien Régime, condemned prisoners were publicly tortured just opposite, in the Place de Grève.

The town Hall. Below : the Place du Châtelet and the St. Jacques Tower.

With the underground Forum which has replaced the old Baltard buildings, with the Georges Pompidou Centre, with its arts galleries, its renovated buildings, and whole streets lined with new businesses drawn here by the excellent prospects, the area around the Halles has undergone a radical change. Strategically placed at the crossing of two lines of the Réseau Express Régional, the railway running deep aground, will this area once again become the "heart of Paris", a rôle that it played during the Middle Ages?

The Georges Pompidou Centre at Beaubourg and the Forum des Halles (below).

The Musée Carnavalet, the turrets of the Manoir de Clisson, the Palais Soubise with the National Archives. The Marais quarter is full of distinguished residences, many of which are now in dire need of restoration.

A detail of the Hôtel Fieubet; the gardens of the Musée Carnavalet; a detail of the Hôtel de Sens and the house of Nicolas Flamel; the National Archives building. Right, a view over the Marais area.

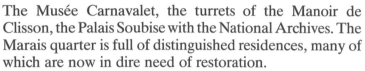

The former Place Royale of Henry IV changed its name to "Vosges" in 1800 in honour of the first *département* to have paid its taxes! This beautifully-laid out square — the oldest in Paris — is bounded by thirty-six buildings all exactly alike, rising up from a series of broad arcades at ground-floor level. The very sloping slate roofs shelter some most elegant dwellings, once occupied by Madame de Sévigné, Marion Delorme, Richelieu, Bossuet amongst others . . . The only one that is open to the public is No. 6, the Hôtel de Rohan-Gueméné, where Victor Hugo lived from 1832 to 1848.

The Place des Vosges. Its façades and arcades.

The Palais Royal houses a number of different activities beneath its roof. In the foreground stands the Comédie Française, then the Conseil d'Etat, the Ministry of Culture, beside the vast gardens, surrounded by apartments raised above an elegant gallery of shops, built by Louis, the architect of the Theatre of Bordeaux. Right, the square block of the Bank of France. In the background, the National Library.

The Palais-Royal.

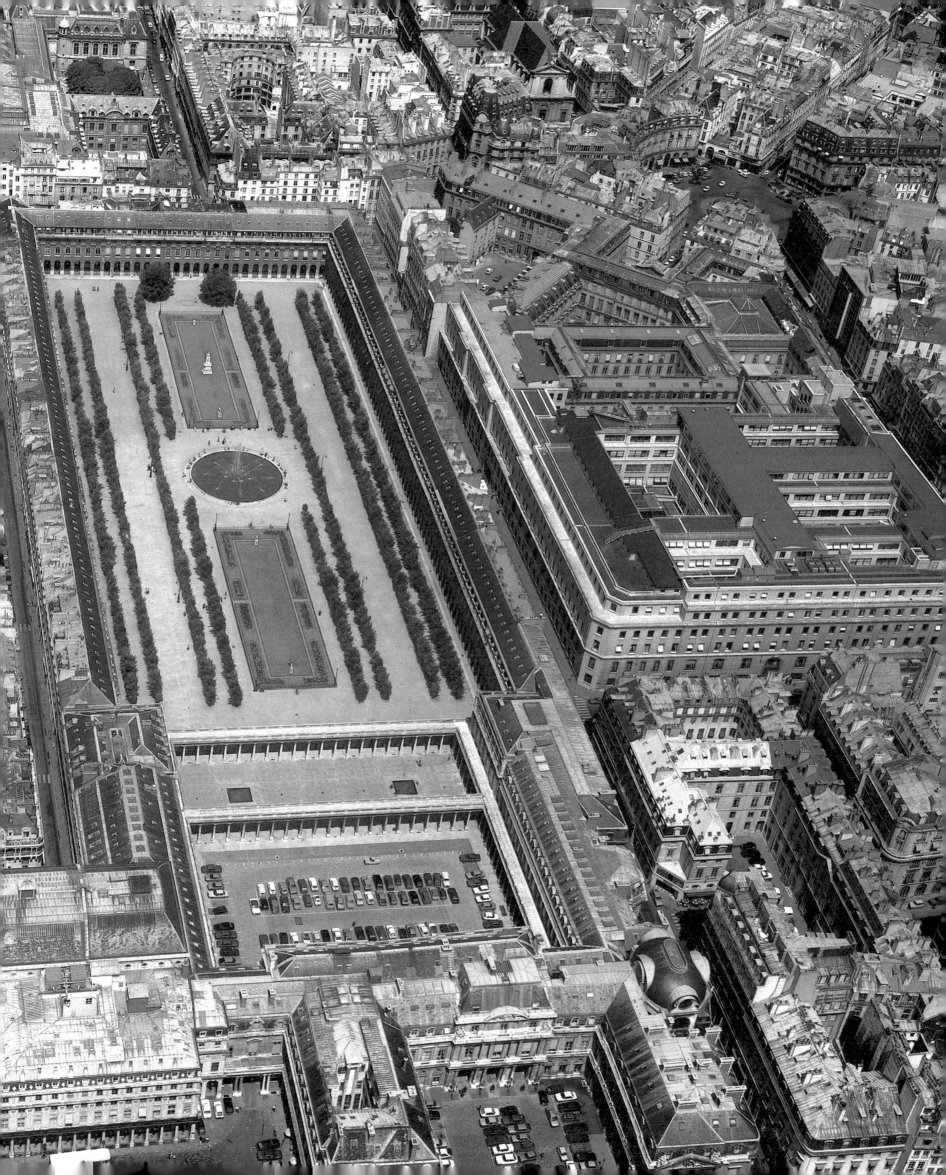

The fountains in the Place du Théâtre-Français, Louis XIV on horseback in the Place des Victoires, and Jeanne d'Arc in the Place des Pyramides . . . The Café de la Paix and the Opera House, built by Charles Garnier.

The Place du Théâtre-Français; the Place des Victoires and the Place des Pyramides. The Opera House, a general view and the great staircase.

Close to the great boulevards, which attract great crowds, stand the National Library, the temple of Knowledge, a haven of culture, and the Stock Exchange, where day after day the ups and downs of the economic life of the country are reflected.

The boulevards Montmartre and Poissonnière.

The National Library. The Stock Exchange.

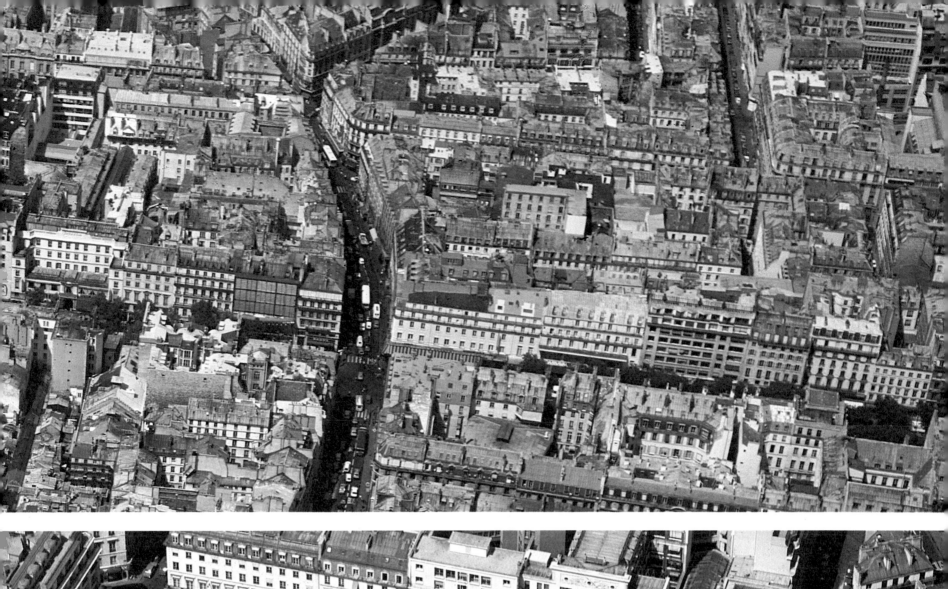

The most famous jeweller's in the world and a hotel that is no less renowned, set into one of the most beautiful architectural sites in the capital, erected according to the plans of the ever-present Mansart: something to add to the glorious achievements of Louis XIV, the glory of Napoleon I being assured by the Vendôme Column, made from the melted down cannons, 1,200 of them, seized at the battle of Austerlitz.

The Place Vendôme and its Column. Great names: Cartier the jewellers' and the Hôtel Ritz nearby.

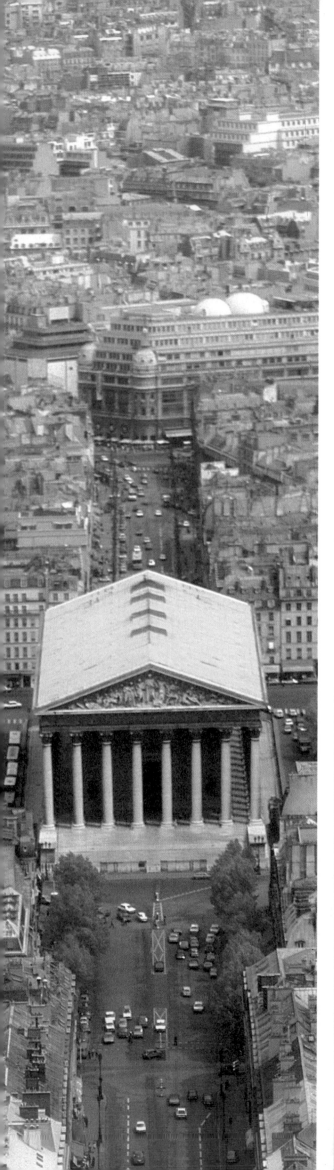

The false Greek temple of the Madeleine dates, for the most part, from the time of Napoleon I. Used as a place of worship only from 1842 onwards, it almost became a station at one time. It was Saint-Lazare, seen in the background, that saved it from this dreadful fate. St. Augustin's reveals another facet of the talent of Baltard. At the opposite end from the Madeleine, in the Rue Royale, that temple of the night world, Maxim's restaurant.

The area around the Madeleine and the church of St. Augustin; below, in the background, the Gare St. Lazare.

The elegant quarter of Monceau and its park with its splendid trees, encircled by fine wrought-iron railings. The pond, surrounded by colonnades, was supposed to recall the scenes of naval battles at the time of Ancient Rome.

Monceau Park.

Pigalle, the Place du Tertre, the bar and restaurant of the Lapin Agile (or "A Gilles"?): the mound of Montmartre, touristically very well organized around that rival of the Eiffel Tour: the Sacré-Coeur.

The Place Pigalle and the Place du Tertre; the "Lapin Agile"; the la Galette Mill. The Sacré-Cœur and its gardens.

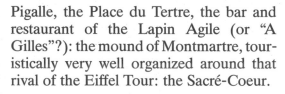

The usual route for popular marches goes from the Bastille to the République. The Saint-Martin canal, which runs underground, passes under the Génie de la Colonne.

The République, the *Génie* of the Bastille and the St. Martin Canal. The Place de la Bastille.

In less than three decades, the Maison de la Radio and the towers of the Front de Seine have determinedly led Paris towards a future that the Statue of Liberty (the little sister of the one offered by France to the American people, in 1886), rising from the end of the Ile des Cygnes, looks down upon in all its serenity.

The Front de Seine and the Maison de la Radio; below, a replica of the Statue of Liberty.

The Arc de Triomphe seems no more than part of the foreground in this "Horizon 2000", which appears clearly outlined towards the west. The towers of the Défense, the underground complex and its important communications network, go to make up the largest plan of development ever undertaken in the Paris area. 50,000 people live and work there.

Seen from the Arc de Triomphe, the Avenue of the Grande Armée and the towers of the Défense; the area surrounding the Défense.

With its broad avenues, lined with plane trees, and its vast shady parks (here, the Buttes-Chaumont), Paris has managed to remain a fairly green city. Even the new Sports Centre at Bercy has been covered with a lawn. 425,000 trees and 2,830 hectares of parkland, woodland and gardens keep a staff of 400 workers permanently occupied. And very successful they are too, it seems. The locust-tree in the Plant Garden and the false acacia of St. Julien-le-Pauvre were planted in 1601, while the plane tree in Monceau Park is slowly but surely moving towards its seven-meter circumference.

The Observatory and Denfert-Rochereau; the Sports Centre at Bercy. Right : the Buttes-Chaumont.

Friends of Nature will seek a peaceful spot in the Bois de Boulogne or the Bois de Vincennes, to the west and to the east of the capital. The country is delightful and their lakes much sought after. The Bois de Boulogne also boasts fine sports fields, a zoo and a magnificent rose-garden.

The lake in the Bois de Vincennes. This page, the Bois de Boulogne : the rose-garden, a trip on the lake, the waterfall.

Last page : St-Germain-l'Auxerrois, "parish of the kings of France", a view of the Louvre, the quayside near the Seine, one end of the Pont-Neuf : in the heart of Paris.

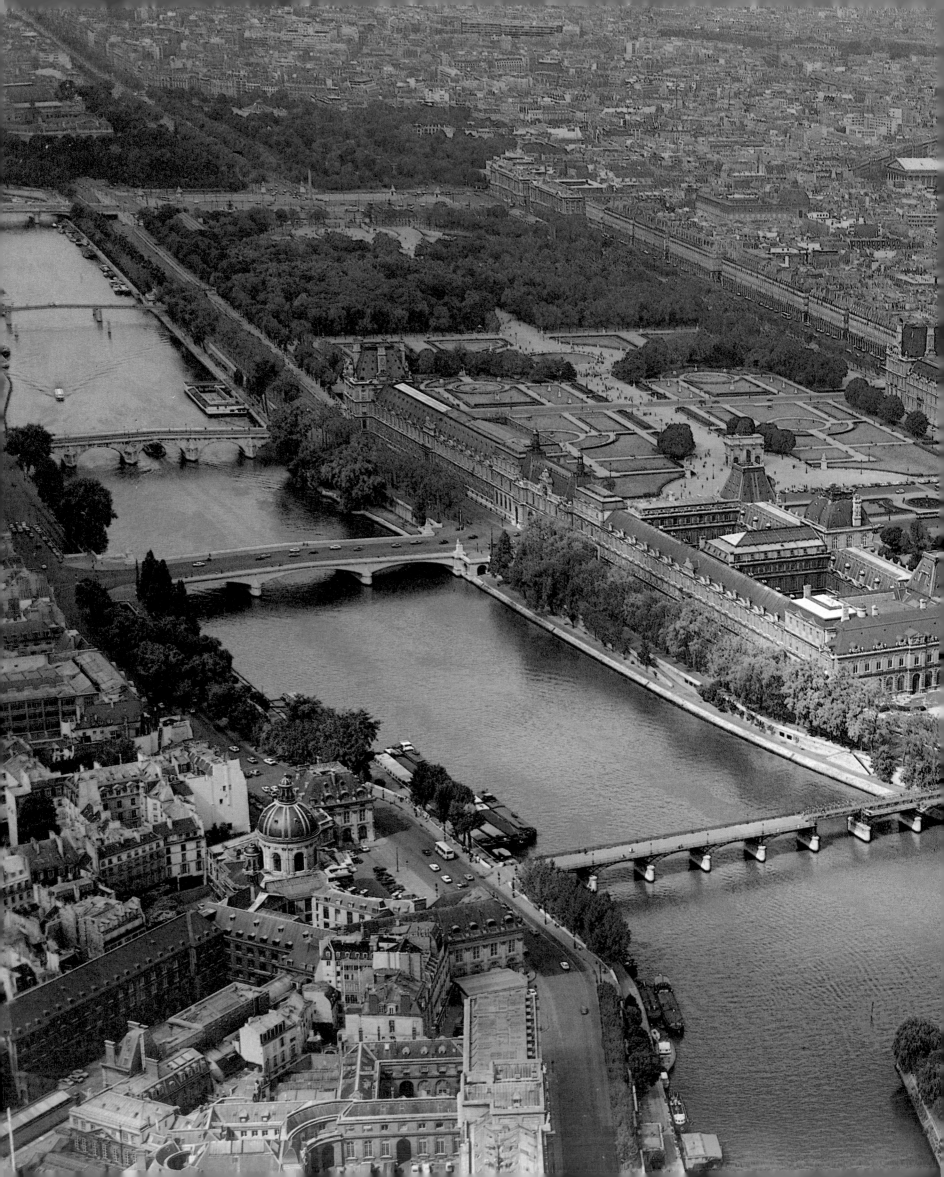